Wolfgang Amadeus Mozart

REQUIEM

K 626

Vocal Score/*Klavierauszug*

edited by/*herausgegeben von*
RICHARD MAUNDER

Contents/*Inhalt*

The full score is also on sale. Full scores, vocal scores, and instrumental parts are available for hire from the publisher's hire library.

Music Department
OXFORD UNIVERSITY PRESS
Oxford and New York

REQUIEM
K 626

Edited by
Richard Maunder

W. A. MOZART
(1756–1791)

[1] Requiem aeternam

Printed in Great Britain

OXFORD UNIVERSITY PRESS, MUSIC DEPARTMENT, GREAT CLARENDON STREET, OXFORD OX2 6DP

Segue

[2] Kyrie

[3] Dies irae

[4] Tuba mirum

[5] Rex tremendae

* ♪ ♪♪ ♪♪ ♪ throughout for voices in original (see full score).

24

Requiem

[6] Recordare

[7] Confutatis

*♩. ♪ in original (see full score).

Segue

[8] Lacrymosa

Segue

[9] Amen

[10] Domine Jesu

Requiem

Requiem

[11] Hostias

(SANCTUS) TO PAGE 73

[12] Agnus Dei

Segue

[13] Lux aeterna

[14] Cum sanctis

APPENDIX
Two movements by F. X. Süssmayr (1766–1803)

[15] Sanctus

Requiem

[16] Benedictus

Processed and printed by
Halstan & Co. Ltd., Amersham, Bucks., England